THE MIRROR WALL

Also by Richard Murphy

SAILING TO AN ISLAND
(1963)

THE BATTLE OF AUGHRIM
(1968)

HIGH ISLAND
(1974)

THE PRICE OF STONE
(1985)

NEW SELECTED POEMS
(1989)

About Richard Murphy

RICHARD MURPHY:
POET OF TWO TRADITIONS
Maurice Harmon, editor
(Wolfhound Press, 1978)

RICHARD MURPHY

The Mirror Wall

BLOODAXE BOOKS

Copyright © Richard Murphy 1989

ISBN: 1 85224 092 X hardback edition
       1 85224 093 8 paperback edition

First published 1989 by
Bloodaxe Books Ltd,
P.O. Box 1SN,
Newcastle upon Tyne NE99 1SN.

Published simultaneously in Ireland
by Wolfhound Press, Dublin, and in North America
by Wake Forest University Press, North Carolina.

Bloodaxe Books Ltd acknowledges
the financial assistance of Northern Arts.

Typesetting by Bryan Williamson, Manchester.

Printed in Great Britain by
Bell & Bain Limited, Glasgow, Scotland.

Acknowledgements

The Government of Sri Lanka granted me permission in 1987 to use copyright material by the late Professor Senarat Paranavitana in writing these poems. I acknowledge this debt with gratitude. *Sigiri Graffiti* by S. Paranavitana was published in two volumes by the Oxford University Press for the Government of Ceylon in 1956, and reprinted at the Government Press in Colombo in 1983.

I am thankful to Nihal Fernando for the four photographs of the frescoes (pp. xvii-xx), and to Luxshmanan Nadaraja for the sample of a Sinhala poem written on the Mirror Wall. The cover photograph of a cloud nymph, painted on a rock at Sigiriya in the 5th century, is reprinted by permission of UNESCO.

The lotus, sapu flower, jasmine, bo leaf, lion, elephant, swan, makara and other Sri Lankan emblems were drawn by Mandalika Manjusri.

I am grateful to several writers who helped me to work on these poems in Sri Lanka. Ashley Halpé, Professor of English at Peradeniya University, introduced me to the *Sigiri Graffiti*, showed me some of his own versions and encouraged me to persevere. Anuradha Seneviratne, Professor of Sinhala at Peradeniya, gave me instruction on the Old Sinhala texts, including their background, and critical advice on my adaptations. Senake Bandaranayake, Professor of Archaeology at

Kelaniya University and Director of the Sigiriya Project, provided me with much information and special access to the Mirror Wall and the Frescoes. An essay by P.B. Meegaskumbera of Peradeniya University influenced my response to several lyrics.

Also, I am grateful to the editors of *Grand Street* and the *Times Literary Supplement*, in which many of these poems first appeared; and to the editors of the *New York Review of Books*, in which the poem called 'Sri Lanka' was published.

The British High Commissioner to Sri Lanka, David Gladstone, and his wife April, sponsored a performance of these poems, with music by Lalanath de Silva, for two hundred guests at Westminster House, Colombo, on 24 March 1988.

Finally, a word of thanks to my native country. My work on *The Mirror Wall*, requiring long visits to Sri Lanka, was continuously and generously supported by Aosdána, the Arts Council and the Department of Foreign Affairs in the Republic of Ireland.

Contents

The numbers in square brackets refer to the Old Sinhala songs in *Sigiri Graffiti* by S. Paranavitana.

Sri Lanka

Being nearly heart-shaped made me seem a ham
   On early spice trade navigators' charts
   Tinctured with cinnamon, peppered with forts,
To be eaten up under a strong brand name
Like Taprobane, Serendib, Tenarisim –
   Copper-palmed lotus island slave resorts –
   And I succumbed to lordly polished arts
That cut me down to seem a white king's gem,
A star sapphire tear-drop India shed
   On old school maps, a lighthouse of retorts
Flashing from head to head. My leonine blood
Throbbed wildly when resplendent freedom came
   Mouthing pearl tropes with Pali counterparts,
Exalted, flawed; and made me seem as I am.

Preface

Much of my happy childhood was spent in Ceylon, where my father was the last British Mayor of Colombo. After a gap of fifty years, I returned to Sri Lanka, and found the inspiration for these poems. It came from songs written in Old Sinhala during the 8th, 9th and 10th centuries. The original holographs remain on the curving, parapet wall of a footpath half way up the rock fortress of Sigiriya in the central province. The wall is about a hundred metres long, and over two metres high. Incised with metal styles in the polished plaster, the songs relate to mysterious, "golden" women in frescoes painted on the undulating rock above this "mirror wall", who seem to be dancing in the clouds. Twenty of these portraits have survived since the end of the 5th century.

Sigiriya, or *Sihigiri* in Old Sinhala, means 'Lion Rock': and the Sinhala people are the 'lion' people, mythically descended from a lion who raped an Indian princess. From some directions, the rock resembles a crouching lion that has lost its head: and from others, a massive lingam, the symbol of Shiva. Rising 600 feet above the forest, tanks and paddy fields of the peneplain, it stands on the island's main water parting, where the rivers that flow east into the Bay of Bengal part from those that flow west into the Indian Ocean.

Sigiriya was fortified by a king called Kassapa or Kasyapa, who reigned there from AD 477 to 495, the only king of Lanka to have done so. The *Mahāwamsa*, an ancient Theravada Buddhist chronicle written in Pali, accused Kassapa of slaying his father by having him sealed up in a niche inside a wall: and said that he chose Sigiriya 'through fear', because the rock 'is difficult of ascent for human beings. He cleared [the land] round about, surrounded it with a wall and built a staircase in the form of a lion. Thence it took its name...Then he built there a fine palace, worthy to behold, like another Ālakamandā and dwelt there like Kuvera.'

Kuvera was the god of wealth in the Hindu pantheon, and Ālakamandā, or Alakā in Sanskrit, was the city he occupied on the mythical Mount Kailāsa in the Himalayas. The Sanskrit poet Kālidāsa, who lived a century before Kassapa, alludes to Kailāsa as 'the mirror for goddesses', and to Alakā as adorned with paintings he compares to the cloud's rainbow. Four of the Sinhala songs refer to the women in the frescoes as *asaran*, from *apsaras* in Sanskrit, the cloud nymphs who frequented Kailāsa. One song suggests they were the king's five hundred wives. Were they 'stuck to the rock' as offerings to Kuvera or the Lion or the local mountain god? Perhaps their function was to ensure sufficient rainfall to grow rice in this dry zone: rain was sometimes regarded as the semen of the gods.

After Kassapa was defeated in battle by his half-brother, Sigiriya was abandoned as a royal residence, but greatly revered as a place of secular pilgrimage. People were drawn there from all over Sri Lanka and southern India for the next seven hundred years. Eventually the ruins were smothered in jungle, until the site was opened up in the last century.

Some of the writers signed their names on the wall, declaring their rank, profession and place of residence. They were members of a feudal nobility and its entourage; officials, merchants, clerks and Buddhist monks. Only two of the authors professed to be 'poets'. At least twelve poems were written by women. Monks had occupied Sigiriya centuries before Kassapa's reign, and remained for centuries thereafter. In some of their puritanical songs, they condemned the fresco nymphs as faithless wives or prostitutes or dancing girls. Theravada Buddhism never encouraged erotic art or sensual passion.

The women in the pictures were seen by the writers from various contradictory points of view, but never rearing children. War, famine, plague, or what we might call reality, did not enter into their stylised world. Nor was it necessary to describe what could be seen on the spot. In Old Sinhala, as in Sanskrit poetry, it was more important for writers to celebrate and affirm their culture than to be original or subversive. No song implies that Kassapa was a parricide, though several argue about his wives' behaviour after his death. There is no definitive version of why the women are on the rock, or what they are doing, or who they are: and the songs grow from this fertile mystery.

Called *gi* in Sinhala, the lyrics were sung, perhaps with vina, flute and drums, in the gallery under the portraits where they were written. There are poems about love, rejection and the separation of lovers; satires and complaints; joyful, erotic celebrations; and rueful ironies. Much of the writing is light verse or vers de société. There is at least one prose inscription, which says: *I am Budal, I came in company and saw Sihigiri. Many people who saw [Sihigiri] have written verses. I therefore did not write one.*

The forms of the *gi* are syllabic: usually 38 to 43 syllables, divided into two lines, each of which contains a "breath", or caesura, after 9, 10, or 11 syllables. An English quatrain could match this, but Sinhala verse has no stresses. End rhymes are rare, though internal rhyming, assonance and alliteration frequently occur. Some short Sinhala words can have several meanings that deepen the ambiguity, or the irony of a lyric.

A few of my poems are versions that keep close to the syllabic count and meaning of their Old Sinhala sources. But more often I use a variety of freer forms to elaborate images and ideas evoked by the sources; to bring in modern voices; to include some description and context; or to combine material from several songs. My sources are among the 685 songs that were transcribed, edited, translated and introduced by Senarat Paranavitana in his *Sigiri Graffiti*, a two volume masterpiece of Sinhala scholarship, which informed and inspired my work.

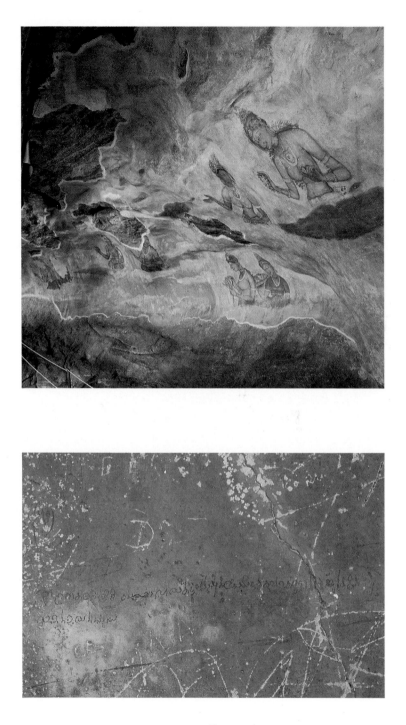

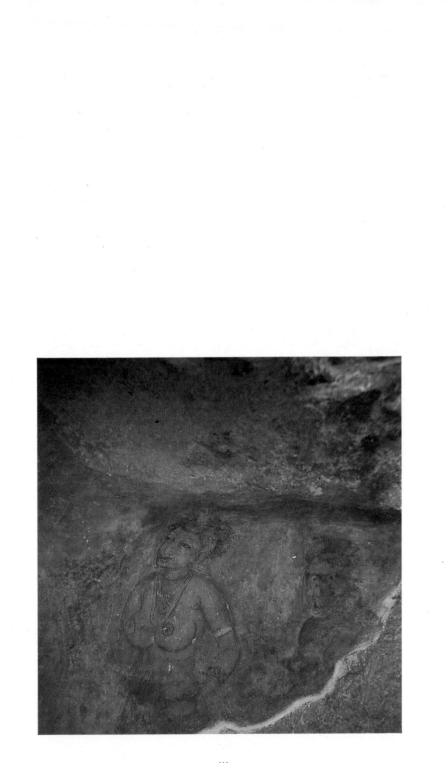

xviii

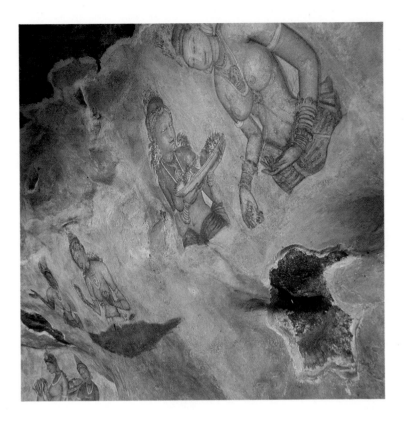

Invocation

All you feel on the Lion Rock won't come
by breathing heavily.
Take up a style

And let the Rain Girls give you airs to lift
songs from the scores
that pierce the Mirror Wall.

KASSAPA

Perhaps the king, whose name evoked the sun,
Riding his elephant, under a pearl umbrella,
Through parched rice-fields on the dry zone plain,

Had seen this rock aspiring from the earth
To penetrate the clouds loafing in heaven:
And put five hundred of his virgin brides,

Dressed in cascades of jewellery, to make
A splash on the summit, and entice the gods
To cast their semen on the ground as rain:

Then shone here, as the god of wealth, supreme
In rice and gems, going about on three legs,
Devising arts to give the gods sublime

Erections that would last: broad galleries
Of golden girls the rock itself embraced
Inside a wall whose mirror caught their souls:

And sheathed the rock-head in a lion mask
To father a strong race, out of whose mouth
At festivals he made great fountains pour.

Falling and falling
        through feverish jungle
with leeches sucking our blood,
pythons dangling from creepers
        over the footpath,
leopards in ebony trees
        looking us in the eyes,
        and herds of wild elephants
trumpeting on our tracks,

We found our way exalted
        by this massive monolith,
and began as we climbed
to love each other better,
        leaping into fountain tanks
        to quench fiery thirst.
Our thanks to the Lion
        who protects Sri Lanka
for sparing us one glorious day.

Climbed up the Lion Rock
    and met the King himself:

Bricked alive in the mountain
    with a lion face of brick.

His power house odour
    induced feverish sweat.

We stepped through his open jaws
    and came out on top,

Where earth's wheel is joined
    to the great wheel of heaven:

A sky palace water tower
    whose old courses cracked.

His rain girl collection filled
    the rock's driest hollow.

Coming up the mountain track
               singing a song
    I never got a word
         from the golden girls
  kept here by their lover
                   endlessly apart:

    so I poked around the Lion Rock
        and was stunned.

Look, my darling, how the people
Who chatter to each other
Lightening the hard way up

Are drawn without a word
To a woman whose beauty
Irradiates the silence of the rock.

The king's palace rock is delectable –
          or so I had always heard,
and a picture had formed in my mind.
Now on the spot. I think I will need
          more eyes than the stars
for my mind not to go completely blank.

All over the Lion Rock
          the king had his women
fixed up as water nymphs
          pretending this was heaven:

And hared off to look
          for salvation as a turtle
seeking throughout the ocean
          for a yoke to fit his neck.

'I'm dying,'
the king thought,
a while before
having to leave this world.
He couldn't take
his wives,
all tarted up in rich distemper.
'Hang on,'
he jeered at them,
'and fuck the rock!'

Who got angry,
      you or your husband,
            (the same word can mean *lord*),

In a song by Mital,
      'slovenly written in script
            attributable to the ninth century'?

Were you happy climbing
      to the mountain top,
            or dragged by your hair?

'The writing is blurred
      by the weathering of the plaster,
            and scribbles of later visitors.'

You leapt down, they said.
      Mital was not sure:
            you could have been thrown.

Did you dance on the terrace
      that hot blustery day
            too close to the precipice,

While the king, smoking ganja,
      sat calm as a lotus
            on a solid rock-crystal divan?

Mital does not mention,
    because Yagi verse is too spare,
        your opulent jewellery:

The oval aquamarines
    above and between your breasts,
        the ponderous gold ear-rings,

And armlets adorned
    with cats' eyes and chrysoberyls
        which kept you chained;

Or the rope of pearls
    hung round your neck enslavingly.
        He refers obliquely

To a tree called *kolomba*,
    (a bad, or a grieving, mother?),
        able to survive

Teetering on the rock-edge
    with roots going far down the cliff
        clinging to every moist crevice.

He leaves you in his poem
    branching out and blossoming
        as you fall to this day.

When spoken to
        never to speak
a word to anyone
        and to keep to our rock.

This irrevocable oath
        they all had to take
before the king's death
        when those forest girls were stuck

On the mountain, skin dyed
        to look golden. Hard luck!
It was a royal
        Old Sinhalese trick,

Making a political
        pun to lock
the gold girls up in a vocable
        meaning *word* and *rock*:

Letting the public try
        by seductive lyric
to break them free
        of their graphic mental block.

Longing
to sing
and play
music
she'd brought the lute
up to her shoulder
when
the king's death
struck a chord

and being as good as gold
didn't she strike the lute
to smithereens.

Her loose appearance may give offence,
But I'll stand up for her innocence.

When told that her prince was dead
She tore off her flowery tiara.

The blossom in her hand isn't beckoning:
It happened to fall from her head.

They deck you
with love-making flowers
arrange your hair
to fall in seductive tresses
put waterlilies
and a sapu bud in your hand

Now
fair girl
you are ready
for them to attach you
to the dark rock
for ever

Some of the figures
look painfully deformed:
all their lustre
has long been dimmed.

These were pliant girls
who had a good time
in their time
when somebody was fond of them.

Good Luck!

I love to climb up here at dawn, and stand
looking at lotus flowers
blossoming from a cut stone mountain pond:
while a gentle breeze, carrying a scent
from nowhere to nowhere
comes across
and overpowers my mind.

I am Lord Agboy, I wrote this verse.

Adorable mountain girl
With your dark blue waterlily eyes
And red-hot hand bearing a lotus
You took my mind
Away from another person
By sweet brute force.

You who remain
fresh on the rock
may think:

'In our endless youth
surviving here
we've never met

a man we could love
who did not die
when slain.'

With her hair tied up in flowery ringlets
And a blue tilak mark on her forehead,
The most hunted gold creature on the mountain
Catches you with her eyes in a perfect snare.

Women like you enable people
To say just what they think:
At Sigiri
You compelled my hair to bristle,
My whole body rose up thrilled.

Does the blue waterlily or the purple lotus
Resemble the motionless iris in your eyes?
How distant is your vision?
Is our life still comparable to your still life?

In
Your eyes
The lustre that pours down
From a candle in a bowl of jewels blazes.
The stillness in that flame can't be contrived.
Your nature is well shown
To be divine.

Your eyes
have turned into waterlilies:
beautiful,
but I can't rejoice.

I was not good enough
in my past life
for you to grant me
a word in this.

Eyebrows midnight blue.
A swan
Is mooning down
The milky lake of her breast.

Her waist
Is a mere waterdrop.
Luminous rainbow fish
Laze in the coral of her lips.

And here she lies
Revealing herself
As a goddess
Confronting you now.

No, don't look at her!
Let's go away.
The golden figures
With wet-nurse breasts
Should be hacked off.
Captivating men
On a flaking wall
High up the hill
They are unspeakable!

I am Friar...
(*the name is blurred by weathering...*)

Picture a palm tree
with bunches of golden nuts
full of milk
always ready
in a hundred small ways to be used.

How much better it will thrive in a clump
on a low stretch of water
than high and dry on its own out of reach.

Instead of you flaunting
your golden bosoms
like bunches of prostitutes
on this ruinous wall
you should be put in a neighbourhood museum.

I'm Bati
a young widow
climbing Sigiriya
looking for words
to stitch into a song.

No song of mine
purled on moonstone
will gratify ladies
who use their long eyes
to sew people up.

Beyond looking brilliant
Have they nothing in mind?
You men call them faithless.
Didn't your gold brushwork
Make them what they are?

A woman wrote this for women
Sealed in the rockface
As gems on show to the crowd.
Their star sapphire eyes
Look far too bright to be touched.

I was in paradise
     where nymphs in spotless health
Cavorted on the generous clouds
     to please the god of wealth.

Up jumped my hand across
     a bamboo moral hurdle
In a rich desire to sport
     with the pearl string of a girdle.

Her hand
     is given like water
     to those thirsting for love
     that will last.

The eye
     she cast
     when given my love
     was dry as blue paint on old mortar.

Superlative make-up artist,
   please tone down
the blues of your lily-petal eyes,
   and close
the gem boutique of your mouth
   full of fake pearls.
Stop posing on the cliff-top:
   show more heart!

Yes
She is beautiful
And may have once done good
But by not following the correct path
Because she was lacking in faith
She cannot warm to people
So keeps to herself
Her almost
Burnt out
Heart

25

She's planting
the seeds
of a marketable
gingered melon smile:

Chatting
with a voice
that squeezes me a juice
labelled 'keep cool':

Slitting
her eyes
to let me savour
two segments of blue shell:

Pouring
on my flash
of burning hope
her laugh like perfumed oil.

From Hunagiri Temple
I've come with all I possess:
Needle, fan, begging bowl
And my robe as a novice.

A person much talked about
Lives up in that cave, whoring.
Be wakeful in thought:
Guard the door of hearing!

She spreads a broad grin
Round a soul she's devouring.
Terrible thing to have seen.
I can't stop shuddering.

No! You must not believe
Those beauties you can see
In that sheltered grotto
Are happy or good or true.

Remember
The world is passing away
The world is suffering
The world has no identity.

Just let me creep away
if I get this wrong:
scratch out my name
on the wall at Sigiri!

I'm Dayal Bati, a woman
visiting the rock,
this great lady's home;
wrapping a song for her.

'What seed or fruit
did those who stayed on here
succeed in gathering
from the rays of the moon?

To whom did the beam
she shone in the morning
not bring a ray
of mounting happiness?'

Does a good lover
      have to become
the lover of goodness
      in a noble woman?

The tide in the ocean
      cannot stand still:
when the full moon has risen
      it must rise.

She stopped me feeling sad.

Then took off
to the rugged peak of a mountain precipice.
Joined a happy commune.
Everlasting, indeed!

Why can't I simply fall asleep?

Thinking endless thoughts
about someone you madly desire
can become not very becoming.

It would be nice to stop craving
that one with lascivious eyes
and to think of her as your sister.

The song of Lord Sirina of Digalavana

My Lord,
    the Cloud!
        I worship you
        for bringing seed
    from heaven
to the earth.

Go to the house
    of a woman
        whose heart is broken:
        her tongue and lips
    are dry
with despair.

Rain healing
    compassion
        to restore her love:
        speak to her,
    keep speaking,
make it flow!

Pure as the hare with spots
mindfully drawn
by the king of the gods
on the mandala of the moon,

I wish you could stay
for a thousand years as you were
that singular day
you starred in my mental sphere.

I looked
    and my wish was granted:

Years of longing anxiously
    ended at Sigiri in joy.

The girl I'd wanted
    was planted in front of me

Immovable as the rock
    turning her body into gold.

She couldn't speak:
    there was nothing I could say.

D

The virtue of this breeze,
         enriched with jasmine,
    giving pleasure to us all,

Comes from the women,
         pictured as lianas
    bending under the opulent

Burdens of their breasts,
         who linger on the edge
    of the precipitous rock,

Faithful to their lover
         in endless separation,
    eyes fixed on the road,

While dancing in reflections
         along the mirror wall
    waving yellow yak-tail fans.

Doesn't the Sanskrit "apsaras",
Going between the waters of the clouds,
Describe these nymphs as they are painted here
For born lovers, like us?

O milkmaids of the cosmos
Take me as I come within your scope
Non-violently: for I will disturb you no more
Than a breeze trembling in moonlight.

The moon rose
    when I was on the mountain
    looking closely
at those eyes like a forest gazelle's.

Climbing down
    I resolved to lure them
    nightly to gleam
across my memory's water-hole.

Their small elliptical
    dying-of-thirst flame
    made all seem dark
until this poem came to light.

The wet monsoon
    came to us in a thunderstorm
    bursting with relief.

Clay pots and brass bowls
    overflowed with drips
        from leaks in broken roofs.

Hundreds and thousands
    of trees like birthday cake candles
        were lit in a flash and blown out.

Tuna and seer-fish
    got whirled into the sky
        and landed among spice gardens.

A curlew felt cheated
    and left the country
        filing a wretched complaint.

From the summit of parched hills
    waterfalls roared
        like tomtoms beaten in temples.

In our cots at night we crowed
    when firefly swarms kept bringing
        miniscule buds of light.

You, with your eyes half closed
    as a nymph on the Lion Rock
        stirred up these airs.

If we'd known the secret
    of sapu flowers at your fingertips
        would it have helped?

Wow! That girl on the mountain
has bound in Sri Lankan style
your eyes and your soul.

How? By showing you her breasts
curved as a Sinhala "O"
swanning on the mirror wall.

Bow to their beauty, as they float by,
drunk for a thousand years
on the nectar of lotuses.

O no! Don't go from the mountain side
    now that I've just come.

Stay as my nymph, while I still adore you,
    in poor shape as I am.

You're my waterlily woman on the rocks,
    my mother in a rain-cloud,

My mango sweetheart tongue to tongue,
    and my lightning rod in bed.

If you examine the way
women were poised here embracing the rock
and how they are now dropping down
off the cruel stony face,

You may from this angle
notice a necklace loosening its thread
and follow with your eyes
a scattering of pearls.

A melon-pip smile
        pops out from under
a dense thundercloud of hair,

Sending the shivers
        through flowers that cling
to its wavering tendrils.

After being struck twice
        by sheet lightning I saw
a housewife's face closing up.

Becoming attached
	to one of these colourful
Wallflower girls
	who have such fetching eyes,

Is like being stitched
	into the body of a poem
With a gaping wound
	that won't heal in your mind:

Or like jewelling the hook
	that's used by a mahout
To master an elephant
	and jabbing it in your head.

How can that dancer,
	whose eyes half shut
	are like slender greeny carp,
	cool our passion

With garlands hung
	as fishnets drying
	on the coral pink
	atolls of her breasts?

As a woman I'll gladly
          sing for these women
who are unable to speak.

You bulls come to Sigiri
          and toss off little lovesongs
making a big hullabaloo.

Not one has given us
          a heart-warming sip
of rum and molasses.

Maybe none of you thought
          we women could have lives
of our own to get through.

He kept coming back to look:
    it was her colour
        that struck him.

She was black,
    and stood out
        on the mountain

With golden girls
    embracing her
        as a sister.

Once he'd imagined them
  how could the portrait painter cope
    with his own inextinguishable
      desire to depict

These joyful brides of the mountain
  inside whose formless dark
    their waists, slender as lightning,
      glitter and connect?

Crushed
by ill treatment
she had to change her life.

Her mouth
tasted of ashes
from the burning in her breast.

Her eyes
had no more tears to shed:
she was written off as a woman.

They turned her
into a damsel with a tail
as pliable as the lash of a whip.

I am Kitala: I wrote this.

Whoever it was who wrote
    on the mirror wall
    at this high level
    will never be known.

Yet another guy came
        and improperly boasted
    the winning song
    had been written by him.

A gorgeous peacock alighted
        in a forest glade
    and the dance
    was joined by a cuckoo.

His ploy is to make devices
to home himself in
on your heart.

He bad-mouths honey
as 'floral effluent'
to take it from the plant.

And he reviles
as 'droppings in a cess-pit'
the dearest gems you've got.

This act of his
        in sewing up words
    he thought was making poetry.

He sat down and wrote
        on the reflective wall
    plainly of things we could see.

With no nectar in the sound
        no quicksilver at the core
    it can't be poetry.

When I approach the guarded
                    community of rich widows
          jangling their chunky gold armlets
          on this jungle rock,

My breathing gives me trouble.
               I feel it's much harder
to pull off a poem
          if one is awe-inspired.

Women,
please wave your hands!

One who values my poem
may not exist;
but I'm human.

I've seen the tender moon
in the month of May.

Don't reject me!

The subtle and ethereal
        fluid of the sky
    reflected in the earthy
          pond of the mirror wall

Is as good to look at
        as a beautiful young bride:
    and the women, who are married
        in this picture, act

As if blissfully drunk
        on the flow of nectar
    from songs that reflect their
        beauty, don't you think?

The message I received
            moved me as if a swan
    floating across ruffled
            water had calmed it down.

Love was revived in me
            as if on a lotus bed
    a honey-swollen bee
            had opened bud after bud.

A nectar-soaked bee
    tickled pink
came out of his shell
      and tossing about
    with no restraint
got deeply into a flower.

Humming all day long
    in her short gummy filaments,
  captive to joy
      that never stopped,
    by sunset he was biting
the lotus to let him out.

No,
We do not know
In that empire of the past,
How the heat never made you pour with sweat:

Nor,
When you go
On journeys that last centuries,
How you still keep your courage, and look neat.

'Do we know why that gorgeous creature
lived in a forest community
at that time?'

'At that time
I guess no guy was around like you
with whom she could have some communication.'

The good luck and joy
said to be found
by mounting Sigiri
require a lot of sweat.

Besides these tiptop women
are there not
enough superb bodies
laying on the ground?

While swans are making a smooth passage
from glittering water
to a thicket of lotuses in bud,

A woman picking flowers in the reservoir
is taking my attention
to herself alone: as if I'd come

Through forest to the rock that holds high
our resplendent tradition
merely to tumble into a lotus bed.

After a poem by Governor Nakka,
the Superintendent of Slaves of the Pandyan King.

When our Lion Rock,
        who had offered sacrifice
    by shouldering the city
    of thirty Hindu gods
    with passionless tranquillity,

Asked the Himalayan
        King of Mountains,
    peaked as a lotus cup
    full of gems and gold,
    'was heaven too much for you to bear?'

Meru's disgruntled
        quakings and eruptions
    which had unsettled paradise
    were suddenly
    blown out like a flame.

I don't believe
        there's a ford in paradise
        or a dhobi's shed
        where clothes could be washed.

Water seeps
        through the porous rock
        leaving little enough
        to make the fountains work.

So why does a washerwoman
        climb and mingle
            with the golden caste
        on the sparkling mountain?

She's found a red stain
        on the numinous cloud
        surrounding the loins
    of the king's youngest bride.

Sigiriya, 11 January 1987

Early this morning
　　I walked on the ramparts
　　　　and came across lotuses,

A playful flotilla
　　becalmed on the moat
　　　　hauling white sails down,

As warm rain was falling:
　　each leaf collecting in the palm
　　　　of my hand as a child

Drops that scatter and split
　　like mercury: held very still
　　　　they pool and unite.

*

We were lightly fanned
　　by a friendly wind
　　　　with a scent of jasmine

Around an octagonal pond
　　where the king could recline
　　　　in his pleasure ground

Backed by a huge rock lingam
　　watering a lotus bed
　　　　whenever it rained:

We could see our reflections
    blossoming from the mud
        in fragrant, flamboyant air.

                *

The freshness we found
    near the cobra hood cave
        on white marble steps

Going up to the clouds
    came as kindness from someone
        who usually makes our blood boil:

All the better when we stood
    above the gallery walkway
        between rock and mirror wall,

And watched a transparent
    drop-curtain of rain
        coming down from the gods

By drip-channels grooved
    in the overhanging cliff:
        and saw the violent green

Jungle of the country
    from this high point of love
        diffused through a purifying screen.

If happiness could come by going away
Why did our going away not come at once?
One of the women signalled 'now's your chance',
But gave this writer such a happy glance
That soon she was complaining bitterly
'It's come to look as if they're going to stay.'

'You won't remember this among foreigners
When you've become a foreigner yourself.'

'To think of leaving her, and going away,
Feels like trying to run uphill in a dream.'

Maybe when royalty had gone
And this unhappy girl stayed on,

Ignorant passers by
Insulted her cruelly.

As she'd gone with him all the way
Why was it wrong for her to stay?

On our way
we're scribbling you a line,
dear girls of Ceylon.

Forgive
our coming in such force
to take you in.

Now that we're leaving,
is there a better
way to go?

Entangle,
while you sort out words engraved
as cowries on this mirror
in your mind,

The deep
blue flower that has a clitoris
on a creeper climbing up
a lingam,

With a bright
yellow flower caught in loose hair
rambling along a fragrant hedge
in moonlight:

And remember,
at the last milking of the day
living in Old Sinhala
poetry,

The loving embrace
of a dark young waterlily girl
with a queen whose breasts are like
gold king coconuts,

Coming
together just as daylight
is sinking into the warm ocean
of night.

They came here, looked around, and went,
With this karmic picture
Etched upon their minds.

But they couldn't stop their hands
Wanting to touch
As they climbed and stumbled down.

You salacious people,
Keep your hands off the images!
Don't go giving each breast a rub.

Richard Murphy is one of Ireland's most admired and accomplished poets. Born in Co. Galway in 1927, he spent much of his childhood in Ceylon, where his father was the last British Mayor of Colombo.

Since the publication of his first book, *Sailing to an Island*, in 1963, Murphy has received much praise for such qualities as his 'sureness of direction in the art and a poised and appeased self-knowledge' (Seamus Heaney).

He has published five other books with Faber including *The Battle of Aughrim* (1968), *High Island* (1974) and *The Price of Stone* (1985). The publication of *The Mirror Wall* coincides with the appearance from Faber of Richard Murphy's *New Selected Poems* (1989).